SHEIRIN IS A PRETTY GIRL. SHE IS VERY POPULAR IN HER FIFTH GRADE CLASS.

SHE AND HER FRIENDS ARE INTO HORSES, AND LIKE TO GO OVER TO EACH OTHER'S HOMES TO DRAW THEM, TALK ABOUT THEM, AND PLAY WITH THEM.

HER FRIENDS KNOW THAT SHE IS MUSLIM, AND DO NOT CARE.

SEPTEMBER 11, 2001, SHEIRIN AND HER FAMILY AWOKE...

...TO SEE THE WORLD AROUND THEM CRUMBLE.

THEY ARE SHOCKED AND SADDENED TO SEE SUCH A HORROR.

AT SHEIRIN'S SCHOOL ...

MUSLIMS WERE RESPONSIBLE FOR THE ATTACK. NOW WE ARE AT WAR.

LATER, SHEIRIN'S MOTHER PICKED HER UP FROM SCHOOL.

I DON'T WANT TO BE MUSLIM ANYMORE. I JUST WANT TO BE AN AMERICAN LIKE EVERYBODY ELSE.

LATER THAT NIGHT AT RAMADAN EID UL-FITR DINNER.

MARI, SHEIRIN'S ELDERLY JAPANESE NEIGHBOR, WAS A GUEST AT THE RAMADAN DINNER.

PEACE BE UPON YOU, MARI.

PEACE BE UPON YOU.

SHEIRIN, HOW IS SCHOOL?

THE KIDS TELL ME THAT I'M THE ENEMY BECAUSE I'M MUSLIM.

I DON'T EVEN KNOW WHY YOU'RE HERE. YOU DON'T WANT TO BE SEEN WITH ME.

LET ME TELL YOU WHY I'M HERE. I WISH THAT MY NEIGHBORS HAD COME OUT TO SUPPORT ME WHEN I WAS YOUR AGE.

SIXTY YEARS AGO, AFTER THE JAPANESE BOMBED PEARL HARBOR...

PEOPLE THOUGHT THAT MY PARENTS MIGHT BE SPIES FOR JAPAN.

I SO MUCH WANTED TO LOOK LIKE EVERYONE ELSE! I WAS MAD AT MY PARENTS FOR BEING JAPANESE.

AS I GREW UP, I REALIZED THAT BEING AMERICAN WASN'T ABOUT WHAT I LOOKED LIKE.

IN FACT, MANY YEARS LATER, I LEARNED WHAT IT MEANS TO BE AMERICAN FROM SOMEONE WHO LOOKED LIKE ME.

HIS NAME IS FRED KOREMATSU.

WHO IS HE?

HE WAS AN ORDINARY MAN, WHO DID THE RIGHT THING WHEN THE TIME CAME TO MAKE A CHOICE.

LET ME TELL YOU HIS STORY.

FRED AND HIS GIRLFRIEND IDA ENJOYING A SUNDAY MORNING. SUDDENLY EVERYTHING STOPS.

JAPAN HAS JUST ATTACKED PEARL HARBOR, HAWAII.

THIS WASN'T FRED'S FIRST EXPERIENCE WITH DISCRIMINATION. AS A YOUNG MAN, HE HAD BEEN REFUSED SERVICE ALL ACROSS TOWN.

THE ONLY PLACE FRED COULD FIND SOMEONE WILLING TO CUT HIS HAIR WAS IN OAKLAND'S CHINATOWN.

THE INTERNMENT WAS THE CULMINATION OF A HISTORY OF RACIAL PREJUDICE AGAINST JAPANESE AMERICANS AND OTHER ASIANS, ESPECIALLY IN CALIFORNIA.

THE JAPANESE ARRIVING IN THE UNITED STATES COULD NOT BECOME CITIZENS BY NATURALIZATION, A PRIVILEGE RESERVED TO "FREE WHITE PERSONS" SINCE 1790--AND EXTENDED ONLY AFTER THE CIVIL WAR TO AFRICANS IN 1870.

NEWSPAPERS STIRRED UP ANTI-JAPANESE FEELINGS.

1913: CALIFORNIA PASSES ALIEN LAND LAW, DENYING MOST NON-WHITE ALIENS THE RIGHT TO OWN LAND.

1924: CONGRESS PROHIBITS IMMIGRATION OF MOST NON-WHITE PEOPLE, THEREBY ADDING JAPANESE TO THE LIST OF ALREADY PROHIBITED ALIENS SUCH AS CHINESE AND ASIAN INDIANS.

WHEN WAR BROKE OUT, FRED FELT IT HIS PATRIOTIC DUTY TO FIGHT. HE WENT TO ENLIST ALONG WITH A FEW FRIENDS.

AT THE POST OFFICE, WHERE MEN WENT TO ENLIST, FRED AGAIN FACED DISCRIMINATION.

AFTER BEING TURNED AWAY BY THE MILITARY, FRED CONTRIBUTED TO THE WAR EFFORT BY WELDING SHIPS IN THE OAKLAND SHIPYARD. BUT THAT JOB WOULDN'T LAST.

TODAY'S YOUR LAST DAY. YOU'RE FIRED.

WHAT DID I DO WRONG?

BUT HIS BOSS TURNED AWAY.

IN 1942, FRANKLIN ROOSEVELT SIGNS EXECUTIVE ORDER 9066, AUTHORIZING THE ARMY TO DESIGNATE MILITARY EXCLUSION ZONES. THE ORDER DID NOT SPECIFY JAPANESE AMERICANS, BUT EVERYONE KNEW WHO WAS TO BE EXCLUDED.

"INSTRUCTIONS TO ALL PERSONS OF JAPANESE ANCESTRY. ALL JAPANESE PERSONS, BOTH ALIEN AND NON ALIEN, WILL BE EVACUATED FROM THE DESIGNATED AREA BY 12:00 O'CLOCK NOON TUESDAY, APRIL 7, 1942. ONLY ONE SUITCASE PER PERSON WILL BE ALLOWED."

THE MILITARY JUSTIFIED THE INTERNMENT OF JAPANESE AMERICANS ON "WARTIME NECESSITY." THE MILITARY ARGUED THAT IT WAS IMPOSSIBLE TO TELL A LOYAL JAPANESE AMERICAN FROM A TRAITOROUS ONE. ON THIS LOGIC, ALL OF THEM HAD TO BE SENT TO PRISON CAMPS.

THE MANAGING SECRETARY OF THE SALINAS VEGETABLE GROWER-SHIPPER ASSOCIATION, QUOTED IN THE SATURDAY EVENING POST, OPENLY DECLARED THAT THE DRIVE TO OUST JAPANESE AMERICANS WAS BASED ON RACIAL AND ECONOMIC, NOT MILITARY, MOTIVES: "WE'RE CHARGED WITH WANTING TO GET RID OF THE JAPS FOR SELFISH REASONS ... WE DO. IT'S A QUESTION OF WHETHER THE WHITE MAN LIVES ON THE WEST COAST OR THE BROWN MAN..."

THE ROUNDUP BEGINS. A HUNDRED AND TWENTY THOUSAND JAPANESE AMERICANS ACROSS THE WEST COAST ARE ORDERED TO REPORT TO ASSEMBLY CENTERS. INTERNMENT OF PEOPLE OF JAPANESE DESCENT OCCURS THROUGHOUT THE AMERICAS, FROM PERU TO CANADA. PEOPLE OF JAPANESE ANCESTRY FROM LATIN AMERICA ARE SHIPPED TO THE UNITED STATES FOR INTERNMENT.

MOST JAPANESE AMERICANS REPORTED DUTIFULLY TO THE ASSEMBLY CENTERS, HOPING THEIR OBEDIENCE WOULD PROVE THEIR LOYALTY.

A HUNDRED THOUSAND JAPANESE AMERICANS WERE IMPRISONED BECAUSE OF THEIR RACE?

MANZANAR
★ WAR ★
RELOCATION
CENTER

I WAS ONE OF THEM. I WAS ONLY TWO YEARS OLD WHEN MY FAMILY WAS SENT TO MANZANAR. MY SISTER WAS BORN IN THE CAMP. SHE TELLS PEOPLE SHE WAS BORN IN SAN FRANCISCO, BUT THAT'S A LIE.

WHILE FRED WAS HELPING HIS FAMILY PACK, HIS NEIGHBORS ASKED TO TAKE SOME OF THE FAMILY'S POSSESSIONS.

YOU CAN'T PACK ALL OF THAT IN A SUITCASE! WE CAN TAKE IT.

WHO'LL WATCH OVER MY BUSINESS?

DESPERATE TO STAY WITH HIS GIRLFRIEND, FRED ADOPTED A SPANISH NAME AND UNDERWENT PLASTIC SURGERY ON HIS EYES TO LOOK LESS ASIAN. THE SURGERY DID NOT WORK OUT EXACTLY AS FRED PLANNED.

BEFORE

AFTER

FRED TRIED TO CONTINUE LIVING HIS LIFE AS HE ALWAYS HAD BEFORE.

WHILE IN JAIL, FRED PONDERED OVER HIS TROUBLES.

I WONDER HOW MY FAMILY IS DOING.

WHY HASN'T MY GIRLFRIEND VISITED ME?

WHAT WILL HAPPEN TO THE FAMILY BUSINESS?

FRED'S STORY MADE THE LOCAL PAPER AND THE PAPER WAS PICKED UP BY ERNEST BESIG, ATTORNEY AT LAW.

Francisco Chron

Two Bay Japs Evac Evacuation; Captured

FRED, WHAT THEY ARE DOING IS UNCONSTITUTIONAL.

YES—IN SCHOOL THEY TAUGHT US THAT ALL PEOPLE ARE EQUAL IN THIS COUNTRY, REGARDLESS OF RACE OR RELIGION.

I'M AN AMERICAN, AND INTERNING PEOPLE JUST BECAUSE OF THEIR RACE IS SIMPLY WRONG. I WILL FIGHT THIS ALL THE WAY TO THE SUPREME COURT, IF I HAVE TO.

BUT THAT DOESN'T SEEM AMERICAN! WHAT HAPPENED TO FRED? HE WAS JUST STANDING UP FOR WHAT HE THOUGHT WAS RIGHT. DID HE WIN?

WELL, NOT AT FIRST...

WHILE HE WAITED FOR THE COURTS TO RULE IN HIS CASE, FRED WAS SENT TO JOIN HIS FAMILY AT THE TEMPORARY COMPOUND WHERE JAPANESE AMERICANS WERE FORCED TO ASSEMBLE BEFORE BEING SHIPPED TO AN INTERNMENT CAMP INLAND.

IN THE SAN FRANCISCO BAY AREA, JAPANESE AMERICAN FAMILIES WERE HOUSED IN TANFORAN RACETRACK, MANY IN HORSE STALLS.

41

42

FRED AND HIS FAMILY WERE SHIPPED TO TOPAZ IN THE UTAH DESERT, ALONG WITH 9,000 OTHER INTERNEES. THE CAMP WAS SURROUNDED WITH BARBED WIRE AND HAD SEVEN GUARD TOWERS.

LIFE FOUND A WAY TO GO ON AT TOPAZ.

WHAT COLLEGE WILL TAKE ME NOW?

HIGH SCHOOL CLASS AT TOPAZ

51

EVERY DAY IN SCHOOL, WE SAID THE PLEDGE TO THE FLAG, "WITH LIBERTY AND JUSTICE FOR ALL," AND I BELIEVE ALL THAT. I AM AN AMERICAN CITIZEN. I HAVE AS MANY RIGHTS AS ANYONE ELSE.

FRED, YOU'RE JUST NAÏVE. THIS ISN'T OUR COUNTRY- WE'RE JUST GUESTS HERE.
I DISAGREE. LOCKING US UP ON THE BASIS OF OUR RACE RUNS AGAINST EVERYTHING THIS COUNTRY STANDS FOR. THEY CAN'T DENY LIBERTY WITHOUT DUE PROCESS. AND JUST ORDERING US TO PRISON BECAUSE OF OUR ANCESTRY IS HARDLY DUE PROCESS.
THEY DIDN'T ROUND UP ALL GERMAN AMERICANS OR ALL ITALIAN AMERICANS. THIS IS ABOUT OUR RACE, NOT THE WAR.
YOU'RE RIGHT, FRED, BUT I STILL THINK IT'S BETTER TO KEEP QUIET.
NO, MY FRIEND. WHEN YOU HAVE THE FEELING THAT SOMETHING IS WRONG, YOU MUST SPEAK UP.

ACROSS THE ATLANTIC OCEAN, EVEN GRAVER HORRORS WERE UNDERWAY.

IN EUROPE, A HISTORY OF ANTI-SEMITISM HAD CREATED THE CONDITIONS FOR HITLER TO OFFER A "FINAL SOLUTION" TO THE PRESENCE OF JEWISH PEOPLE IN EUROPE: CONCENTRATION CAMPS FROM WHICH PEOPLE WERE TAKEN TO EXTERMINATION CAMPS.

HITLER ALSO TARGETED ROMA PEOPLE (OFTEN CALLED GYPSIES), MENTALLY ILL AND DISABLED PERSONS, HOMOSEXUAL MEN, FREEMASONS, AND JEHOVAH'S WITNESSES FOR DEATH.

CONGRESSIONAL HEARING.

AMERICA'S TREATMENT OF JAPANESE AMERICANS GAVE THE U.S. A BLACK EYE IN WORLD OPINION. JAPAN APPEALED TO OTHER ASIAN COUNTRIES, EXPLOITING AMERICA'S RACIST TREATMENT OF JAPANESE AMERICANS.

JAPAN'S TRYING TO UNITE ASIA AGAINST US! PROFESSOR DAS, HOW CAN WE STOP THIS?

AS LONG AS ANGLO-AMERICAN POWERS WOULD CONTINUE TO PRACTICE RACIAL DISCRIMINATION AGAINST THE PEOPLES OF THE ORIENT, A VAST MAJORITY OF THE PEOPLE OF ASIA WILL NOT HAVE ANY GENUINE CONFIDENCE IN ANGLO-AMERICAN PROFESSIONS OF PROMOTION OF WORLD DEMOCRACY AND WORLD BROTHERHOOD.

CONGRESS RESCINDED ITS PROHIBITION ON CHINESE IMMIGRATION, HOPING THEREBY TO DEMONSTRATE AMERICA'S OPENNESS TO NON-JAPANESE ASIANS. BUT EVEN THIS CONGRESS DID HALF-HEARTEDLY, ALLOWING ONLY 105 CHINESE PEOPLE TO IMMIGRATE EACH YEAR.

HYPOCRISY UNDERMINED THE ALLIED EFFORT. DURING WORLD WAR II, MUCH OF THE WORLD WAS STILL RULED BY COLONIAL POWERS. IN INDIA, MAHATMA GANDHI LED A MOVEMENT TO FREE THE COUNTRY FROM BRITISH RULE.

SOME IN THE MOVEMENT WANTED INDIA TO SIDE WITH THE JAPANESE IN THE WORLD WAR, ARGUING THAT THE ENEMY OF AN ENEMY IS A FRIEND. GANDHI COUNSELED AGAINST SUCH THINKING.

I HAVE NOTICED THAT THERE IS HATRED TOWARDS THE BRITISH AMONG THE PEOPLE. THE PEOPLE SAY THEY ARE DISGUSTED WITH THEIR BEHAVIOR. THE PEOPLE MAKE NO DISTINCTION BETWEEN BRITISH IMPERIALISM AND THE BRITISH PEOPLE. TO THEM, THE TWO ARE ONE.

THIS HATRED WOULD EVEN MAKE THEM WELCOME THE JAPANESE. IT IS MOST DANGEROUS. IT MEANS THAT THEY WILL EXCHANGE ONE SLAVERY FOR ANOTHER.

OUR QUARREL IS NOT WITH THE BRITISH PEOPLE. WE FIGHT THEIR IMPERIALISM.

IN EARLY 1944, THE ARMY ANNOUNCED THAT IT WAS GOING TO DRAFT YOUNG MEN FROM THE INTERNMENT CAMPS TO CREATE A SEGREGATED UNIT OF NISEI--JAPANESE AMERICANS WHO HAD BEEN BORN IN THE UNITED STATES.

I HEREBY ANNOUNCE THE FORMATION OF THE 442ND INFANTRY REGIMENTAL COMBAT TEAM TO BE COMPRISED OF JAPANESE AMERICANS. AMERICANISM IS NOT, AND NEVER WAS, A MATTER OF RACE OR ANCESTRY.

PRESIDENT ROOSEVELT

TOPAZ DURING PRESIDENT ROOSEVELT'S ANNOUNCEMENT.
THEY'RE OPENING THE DRAFT TO NISEI! THAT MUST MEAN THAT THEY THINK WE'RE REALLY AMERICAN!
I WANT TO SERVE. ALL MY HIGH SCHOOL BUDDIES BACK IN CALIFORNIA ARE IN THE SERVICE.
I'M NOT GOING TO FIGHT FOR THIS COUNTRY WHILE MY FAMILY IS BEHIND BARBED WIRE!
DID YOU HEAR THAT AT HEART MOUNTAIN, SOME GUYS ARE RESISTING THE DRAFT? THEY SAY THAT IF ROOSEVELT WANTS TO DRAFT US, HE HAD BETTER START TREATING US LIKE EQUAL CITIZENS AND FREE OUR FAMILIES.

MAYBE DYING FOR THIS COUNTRY IS THE ONLY WAY WE'RE GOING TO PROVE WE'RE LOYAL AMERICANS.

THE 442ND JOINED THE TROOPS IN EUROPE, LANDING IN ITALY AND PUSHING UP TO HELP LIBERATE SOUTHERN FRANCE. THE REGIMENT BECAME THE MOST DECORATED UNIT IN U.S. MILITARY HISTORY FOR ITS SIZE AND LENGTH OF SERVICE, EARNING THE NICKNAME "THE PURPLE HEART BATTALION." BY THE END OF THE WAR, 33,000 JAPANESE AMERICANS HAD SERVED IN THE MILITARY.

EVEN THE SKIES WERE SEGREGATED.

IN DECEMBER 1944, THE SUPREME COURT RULED AGAINST FRED KOREMATSU. IT BEGAN BY OBSERVING THAT ALL RACIAL CLASSIFICATIONS IN THE LAW MUST BE STRICTLY SCRUTINIZED.

THE COURT CONCLUDED, HOWEVER, THAT THE SELECTION OF PEOPLE OF THE JAPANESE RACE FOR EXPULSION FROM THE WEST COAST WITHSTOOD SUCH DEMANDING SCRUTINY BECAUSE OF MILITARY "NECESSITY."

JUSTICE HUGO BLACK

IT IS SAID THAT WE ARE DEALING HERE WITH THE CASE OF IMPRISONMENT OF A CITIZEN IN A CONCENTRATION CAMP SOLELY BECAUSE OF HIS ANCESTRY, WITHOUT EVIDENCE OR INQUIRY CONCERNING HIS LOYALTY AND GOOD DISPOSITION TOWARDS THE UNITED STATES.

"KOREMATSU WAS NOT EXCLUDED FROM THE MILITARY AREA BECAUSE OF HOSTILITY TO HIM OR HIS RACE. HE WAS EXCLUDED BECAUSE WE ARE AT WAR WITH THE JAPANESE EMPIRE, BECAUSE THE PROPERLY CONSTITUTED MILITARY AUTHORITIES FEARED AN INVASION OF OUR WEST COAST AND BECAUSE THEY DECIDED THAT THE MILITARY URGENCY OF THE SITUATION DEMANDED THAT ALL CITIZENS OF JAPANESE ANCESTRY BE SEGREGATED FROM THE WEST COAST TEMPORARILY."

THE SUPREME COURT WENT ON:
"WE DEEM IT UNJUSTIFIABLE TO CALL THEM
CONCENTRATION CAMPS WITH ALL THE UGLY
CONNOTATIONS THAT TERM IMPLIES."

THAT WAS A LONG TIME AGO. PEOPLE DIDN'T KNOW ANY BETTER.

I WISH IT WERE THAT SIMPLE. IN FACT, THREE JUSTICES DISSENTED IN KOREMATSU'S CASE.

I'LL NEVER FORGET JUSTICE FRANK MURPHY'S WORDS:

"THIS EXCLUSION ORDER FALLS INTO THE UGLY ABYSS OF RACISM. IT RESULTS FROM THE ERRONEOUS ASSUMPTION OF RACIAL GUILT RATHER THAN BONA FIDE MILITARY NECESSITY. I DISSENT, THEREFORE, FROM THIS LEGALIZATION OF RACISM."

WHY DID FRED BELIEVE THAT THE SUPREME COURT WOULD SIDE WITH HIM? THERE WAS SO MUCH RACISM ALL AROUND HIM...

...THE PEOPLE AT THE CAMP WERE RIGHT— HE WAS NAÏVE.

BY THE TIME THE DECISION CAME DOWN, FRED HIMSELF
HAD BEEN PAROLED FROM THE CAMP TO WORK AS A
WELDER IN SALT LAKE CITY. HE HAD TO PROMISE NOT TO
RETURN TO THE WEST COAST.

HE LATER MOVED TO DETROIT, WHERE HE MET AND MARRIED HIS WIFE KATHRYN IN 1946.

THE WAR ENDED IN 1945 AND SOON THEREAFTER JAPANESE AMERICANS WERE FREE TO RETURN TO THEIR HOMETOWNS. THE U.S. GOVERNMENT DECLARED THAT JAPANESE AMERICANS WERE NO LONGER A SECURITY THREAT. FRED AND KATHRYN MOVED TO OAKLAND IN 1949.

IN 1967, FRED'S DAUGHTER KAREN HEARD ABOUT HER FATHER'S CASE FOR THE FIRST TIME FROM A HIGH SCHOOL CLASSMATE'S REPORT.

IN 1944, KOREMATSU LOST HIS CASE. RULING AGAINST FRED KOREMATSU, THE SUPREME COURT UPHELD THE MASS INTERNMENT OF JAPANESE AMERICANS, CITING "MILITARY NECESSITY" AND COUNSELING THAT "HARDSHIPS ARE PART OF WAR."

I COULDN'T AVOID TELLING YOU FOREVER. THAT WAS MY CASE.

YOU AND MOM HAVE ALWAYS TAUGHT US TO LOVE OUR COUNTRY— BUT IT BETRAYED YOU!

THE INTERNMENT ONLY SHOWED ME HOW AMERICAN I AM, HOW COMMITTED I AM TO THIS COUNTRY AND ITS IDEAL OF EQUALITY UNDER THE LAW. WE CAN'T GIVE UP ON THAT.

IN 1981, HISTORIAN AIKO YOSHINAGA—HERZIG AND HISTORIAN PETER IRONS MADE SHOCKING DISCOVERIES WHILE REVIEWING GOVERNMENT ARCHIVES OF THE INTERNMENT. THEIR REVELATIONS WOULD GIVE FRED THE OPENING HE HAD SOUGHT FOR NEARLY HALF A CENTURY TO DEMONSTRATE THE WRONGFULNESS OF HIS CONVICTION.

J. EDGAR HOOVER'S FBI SAID THAT THERE WAS NO EVIDENCE OF JAPANESE AMERICANS ACTING AS SPIES. THE FBI SAID THAT THE INTERNMENT WAS BASED ON PUBLIC AND POLITICAL PRESSURE, NOT MILITARY INTELLIGENCE.

THE ORIGINAL VERSION OF THE GOVERNMENT'S BRIEF TO THE SUPREME COURT IN KOREMATSU V. UNITED STATES IS DIFFERENT THAN THE VERSION THE GOVERNMENT ACTUALLY SUBMITTED. THE ATTORNEY GENERAL WAS ORIGINALLY GOING TO TELL THE COURT THAT THE GOVERNMENT KNEW THAT JAPANESE-AMERICANS DID NOT POSE A THREAT. BUT THEN THEY STOPPED THE PRESSES AND CHANGED THE BRIEF TO SAY THE EXACT OPPOSITE-- THAT MILITARY INTELLIGENCE SUPPORTED THE CLAIMS OF ESPIONAGE BY JAPANESE AMERICANS.

A TEAM LED BY DALE MINAMI AND PETER IRONS REOPENED FRED'S CASE IN 1983.

THEY SOUGHT A WRIT OF ERROR CORAM NOBIS-- AN ACKNOWLEDGEMENT THAT THE SUPREME COURT HAD UPHELD FRED'S CONVICTION BASED ON FACTUAL ERROR. FRED WAS NOW 64 YEARS OLD.

WE ARE HERE TODAY TO SEEK A MEASURE OF JUSTICE DENIED TO FRED KOREMATSU AND THE JAPANESE AMERICAN COMMUNITY FORTY YEARS AGO. THIS IS THE LAST OPPORTUNITY TO FINALLY ACHIEVE THE JUSTICE DENIED THEN.

ASTONISHING EVERYONE, JUDGE PATEL RULED IN FRED'S FAVOR FROM THE BENCH.

THE KOREMATSU CASE STANDS AS A CONSTANT CAUTION THAT IN TIMES OF WAR OR DECLARED MILITARY NECESSITY OUR INSTITUTIONS MUST BE VIGILANT IN PROTECTING OUR CONSTITUTIONAL GUARANTEES. IT STANDS AS A CAUTION THAT IN TIMES OF DISTRESS THE SHIELD OF MILITARY NECESSITY AND NATIONAL SECURITY MUST NOT BE USED TO PROTECT GOVERNMENTAL ACTIONS FROM CLOSE SCRUTINY AND ACCOUNTABILITY. IT STANDS AS A CAUTION THAT IN TIMES OF INTERNATIONAL HOSTILITY AND ANTAGONISMS OUR INSTITUTIONS, LEGISLATIVE, EXECUTIVE AND JUDICIAL, MUST BE PREPARED TO PROTECT ALL CITIZENS FROM THE PETTY FEARS AND PREJUDICES THAT ARE SO EASILY AROUSED.

THE 1983 DECISION PAVED THE WAY FOR A REPARATIONS MOVEMENT, WHICH LED IN 1988 TO AN OFFICIAL APOLOGY AND A PAYMENT OF $20,000 TO EVERY FORMER INTERNEE STILL LIVING.

TITLE I—RECOGNITION OF INJUSTICE AND APOLOGY ON BEHALF OF THE NATION

SEC. 101. The Congress accepts the findings of the Commission on Wartime Relocation and Internment of Civilians and recognizes that a grave injustice was done to both citizens and resident aliens of Japanese ancestry by the evacuation, relocation, and internment of civilians during World War II. On behalf of the Nation, the Congress apologizes.

IN 1998, PRESIDENT BILL CLINTON AWARDED FRED THE NATION'S HIGHEST CIVILIAN AWARD, THE PRESIDENTIAL MEDAL OF FREEDOM.

IN THE LONG HISTORY OF OUR COUNTRY'S CONSTANT SEARCH FOR JUSTICE, SOME NAMES OF ORDINARY CITIZENS STAND FOR MILLIONS OF SOULS-- PLESSY, BROWN, PARKS. TO THAT DISTINGUISHED LIST TODAY WE ADD THE NAME OF FRED KOREMATSU.

AFTER THE TERRORIST ATTACKS OF 9/11, AUTHORITIES BEGAN DETAINING MORE THAN A THOUSAND PEOPLE, MOSTLY MUSLIMS, FOR QUESTIONING.

Balbir Singh Sodhi
1949-2001

BALBIR SINGH SODHI, A SIKH AMERICAN WHO WORE A TURBAN, WAS KILLED IN PHOENIX IN A SPATE OF ATTACKS ON PEOPLE THOUGHT TO BE MUSLIM.

IN HIS 80S, FRED FILED AMICUS BRIEFS BEFORE THE SUPREME COURT IN THE CASES OF GUANTANAMO DETAINEES. THE SUPREME COURT RULED THAT THE DETAINEES HAD A RIGHT TO CHALLENGE THEIR DETENTION IN COURT.

THE END.

Japanese-Americans: A Timeline

1868: The Civil War results in the Four-teenth Amendment, which promises equal protection under the law for all persons.

1882: The passage of the Chinese Exclusion Act leads to demand for labor from Japan.

1885 Feb. 8: The first legal Japanese immigrants land in Hawaii as contract laborers. Between 1885 and 1894, nearly 30,000 Japanese (mostly men) arrive in Ha-

waii to work in the booming sugar plantations. Some choose to move to the continental U.S.

1898: The United States annexes Hawaii, five years after the overthrow of Queen Liliuokalani led by American businessmen.

1899: 26,000 Japanese workers arrive in Hawaii in anticipation of the impending restriction on immigration.

1900: Persons of Japanese descent make up 40% (61,000) of Hawaii's population. The census finds 24,000 persons of Japanese descent on the mainland.

1905: Japanese victory over Russia in war stirs increasing anti-Japanese feeling in United States. The Asiatic Exclusion League is formed in San Francisco, California.

1907: In response to increasing anti-Japanese fervor, the United States and Japan agree to halt Japanese immigration to the United States except for "former residents, parents, wives, or children of residents." In exchange, San Francisco desegregates its schools for Japanese and Japanese-American students.

1910: "Picture brides" start arriving from Japan to marry Japanese men. The decade will see 9,500 Japanese picture brides arrive in Hawaii.

1913: Growing competition from Japanese farmers leads the California legislature to pass an Alien Land Law barring "aliens ineligible for citizenship" from owning land. Many families purchase land through their American-born children (Nisei).

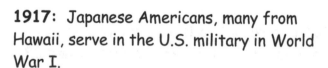

1917: Japanese Americans, many from Hawaii, serve in the U.S. military in World War I.

1919 Jan. 30: Fred Korematsu is born in Oakland, California.

1920: California amends the Alien Land Law to prevent Japanese from purchasing land in someone else's name. It also prohibits non-citizens from leasing land.

1921: Japan stops issuing passports to "picture brides."

1922: Supreme Court declares in *Takao Ozawa v. United States* that Japanese cannot naturalize as American citizens because they are not "white."

1924: Immigration Act of 1924 halts all Japanese immigration to America.

1941 Dec. 7: Japanese planes attack Pearl Harbor naval base in Hawaii. In the following days, more than one thousand promi-nent *Issei* are imprisoned; no charges are filed.

1942 Feb. 19: President Roosevelt issues Executive Order No. 9066, which allows the military to exclude anyone from any area designated as a military zone. This or-der leads to the internment of 120,000 Japanese Americans.

Two-thirds are American citizens. More than half are chil-dren.

Fred Korematsu refuses to report to the assembly center. He changes his name and goes into hiding. He has just turned 23.

1942 Feb. 25: The Navy informs Japanese American resi-dents of Terminal Island near Los Angeles Harbor that they must leave in 48 hours. They are the first group to be removed.

1942 Mar. 2: Public Proclamation No. 1 es-tablishes military exclusion zones 1 and 2 to be complied with Executive Order No. 9066.

Zone 1 includes the western portion of California, Oregon and Washington, and part of Arizona. Zone 2 includes the rest of these states.

1942 Mar. 21: Public Law 77-503 makes a violation of military orders under Executive Order 9066 a federal crime.

1942 Mar. 22: First large groups of Japanese ancestry move from L.A. to the Army-operated Manzanar detention center in the Owens Valley of California.

1942 Mar. 24: The first of 108 military proclamations ordering detention of Japanese and Japanese Americans is issued. By year-end, more than 120,000 are removed from the West Coast designated as military zone 1 and the California portion of zone 2.

1942 May 30: Fred Korematsu is arrested in San Leandro, California. Convicted of violating Executive Order 9066, he is first required to report to the Tanforan Assembly Center in California, and then later moved to the Topaz internment camp in Utah.

1943 Feb. 1: The 442nd Regimental Combat Team is formed, made up entirely of Japanese American volunteers.

1943 Sept. 2: The 100th U.S. Army Battalion composed of Japanese American soldiers from Hawaii lands in Oran, North Africa. It is later known as the "Purple Heart Battalion" for the over 900 casualties it suffers.

1944 Jan. 20: The War Department reinstates the draft for Nisei in detention camps.

1944 June 2: The all-Japanese American 442 Regimental Combat Team (RCT) is sent to the Italian front.

1944 June: The 100th Infantry Battalion merges with the 442nd Regiment.

1944 Dec. 18: Ruling against Fred Korematsu, the Supreme Court upholds the mass internment of Japanese Americans, citing "military necessity" and counseling that "hardships are part of war." In dissent, Justice Murphy denounces the decision as the "legalization of racism."

1945 May 7: Germany surrenders.

1945 Aug. 6: The U.S. drops the atomic bomb on Hiroshima, Japan. Three days later, it drops a second bomb on Nagasaki, Japan.

1945 Aug. 14: Japan formally surrenders and World War II ends.

1945 Sept. 4: Public Proclamation No. 24 revokes exclusion orders and military restrictions against Japanese and Japanese Americans.

1946 March: The last of the ten major detention camps, Tule Lake, in California, closes.

1946 July 15: President Truman receives the 100/442nd Regiment in the White House. He tells the veterans, "You fought not only the enemy but you fought prejudice -- and you have won."

The 100/442nd Regiment is awarded 18,143 Medals of Valor and 9,486 Purple Heart Awards. It is the highest decorated military unit of its size and length of service in U.S. history.

1948 Jan. 19: The U.S. Supreme Court reverses *Oyama v. California*, ruling that California could not bar Japanese American citizen children from owning land.

1948 July 2: President Truman signs the Japanese American Evacuation Claims Act, which was intended to compensate internees for economic losses.

This Act paid less than 10 cents on the dollar for lost property.

1952 Apr. 17: California's Supreme Court holds the state's alien land laws unconstitutional.

1952 June 27: McCarran-Walter Immigration and Nationality Act allows people of all races to be eligible for naturalization. It also establishes a quota system to limit the number of Japanese immigrants to 100 per year.

1965: The Immigration law of 1965 ends national immigration quotas.

1976 Feb. 19: President Gerald R. Ford rescinds Executive Order 9066.

1980: President Jimmy Carter appoints a special commission to investigate the internment of Japanese-Americans during World War II. The commission concludes that the decisions to remove those of Japanese ancestry to prison camps occurred because of "race prejudice, war hysteria, and a failure of political leadership."

1983 June 16: Congressional Commission on Wartime Relocation and Internment of Civilians recommends individual $20,000 payments to internees still living.

1983 Nov. 10: United States District Judge Marilyn Hall Patel hears Fred Korematsu's *coram nobis* action to overturn his 1944 conviction. She reverses the conviction and holds that the internment orders were unconstitutional. Judge Patel writes in the opinion that Korematsu's case "stands as a caution that in times of international  hostility and antagonisms our institutions, legislative, executive and judicial, must...protect all citizens from the petty fears and prejudices that are so easily aroused."

1988 Aug. 10: Congress passes the Civil Liberties Act which grants a reparation check of $20,000 to each living survivor of the internment camps. The figure amounted to $3.36 per day for a detainee who had been interned for two years.

Oct. 19, 1990: Attorney General Richard Thornburgh meets nine elderly Japanese internment survivors to distribute the reparations checks, and he delivers the apology letter from President Bush to them on his knees.

1993 Oct. 1: President Bill Clinton offers a presidential letter of apology to internees and their families. He writes, "I offer a sincere apology to you for the actions that unfairly denied Japanese Americans and their families fundamental liberties during World War II. . . . In retrospect, we understand that the na tion's actions were rooted deeply in racial prejudice, wartime hysteria, and a lack of political leadership."

1998: Fred Korematsu receives the Presidential Medal of Freedom, the nation's highest civilian honor. President Bill Clinton declares, "In the long history of our country's constant search for justice, some names of ordinary citizens stand for millions of souls — Plessy, Brown, Parks. To that distinguished list today we add the name of Fred Korematsu."

2000 Nov. 9: National Japanese American Memorial opens in Washington, D.C. It honors Japanese American veterans and internees of camps in World War II.

2003-2004: Fred Korematsu continues to speak out for basic civil rights. He files amicus briefs in cases, Odah v. United States, Rasul v. Bush, Hamdi v. Rumsfeld, and Rumsfeld v. Padilla, and asks the Supreme Court to review its practice of detaining people indefinitely without formal charges or trials. In his brief for Rumsfeld v. Padilla, Korematsu expresses his concern that "by allowing the Executive Branch to decide unilaterally who to detain, and for how long, our country will repeat the same mistakes of the past."

2005 Mar. 30: Fred Korematsu passes away at the age of 86 in Marin County, California. He is survived by his wife, Kathryn, son, Ken, and daughter, Karen.

2010 Sept. 23: California Governor Arnold Schwarzenegger signs into law a bill making January 30th of every year the Fred Korematsu Day of Civil Liberties and the Constitution.